DISCOVERING

JOHN

by Chris Wiley

PROJECT COORDINATOR
David W. Caudle

COPYEDITOR
Mark K. Gilroy

EDITORIAL ASSISTANTS
Sherry L. Evilsizor
Stacey L. Barker

Copyright 1994
Beacon Hill Press of Kansas City
ISBN: 083-411-4917

CONTENTS

INTRODUCTION
OPENING THE TOOL CHEST

eading is easy; understanding takes work. I trust you are ready to work because to understand John's Gospel, you'll be doing a lot of it. But if you work hard, you won't regret it, for understanding John's Gospel will greatly enrich your life.

One thing I've learned as a carpenter is that the right tools make all the difference. The same is true of mental work. Here are three mental tools that are invaluable in understanding the Gospel of John.

1. A Circle

Think about a line. Some stories are like a line. They move along a straight path. Like a line, they have beginning and ending points, and the point of the story is to get from the beginning to the end. Not too hard to understand.

Now think about circles. Some stories are like a circle; they move round and round. Unlike a line, a circular story ends right back where it began. These stories behave like homing pigeons. The point is to finish where you started.

The Gospel of John is more like a circle than a line. Like a merry-go-round, certain themes keep passing by. And like a giant Ferris wheel, the Gospel contains a stomach-in-the-throat descent (the Incarnation), a head-spinning ascent (the Resurrection), and in between a lot of ups and downs.

2. An Angle

As you read John's Gospel, look for irony. Don't confuse this with sarcasm. They are alike yet very different. While sarcasm is slapstick and can be brutal, irony, in the right hands, is more subtle and powerful. An ironic statement is one in which the literal meaning of the statement is nearly the opposite of what is intended. Composing irony takes a sharp wit and a brilliant mind. Understanding an ironic statement is like a revelation. Getting the point is an "Aha!" experience. This is why John uses it so much. The life of Jesus is filled with ironies.

3. A Point

Finally, keep in mind that all writing is for a point. John's purpose is recorded near the end of his Gospel: "These [things] are written that you may believe that Jesus is the Christ, the Son of God, and that by believing you may have life in his name" (20:31). This Gospel is not the blow-by-blow account of a casual bystander: it is a highly personal and selective rendering of Jesus' life. This means that everything in the story is important because John selected it for a reason. No scrap or tidbit is meaningless.

So open your tool chest, and let's get to work.

HOW TO USE THIS BOOK

This study book has been created with the prayer that the Word of God will find a place in your heart and mind so that you will be equipped to be an effective disciple of Jesus Christ in the midst of the contemporary pagan culture you face each day.

If you are using this study book as a part of a Bible study group, then you are using it to its best benefit. In your group you will learn to trust each other as you discover John and share truths that will help you learn from each other. There is a personal time of discovery to complement each group session, which will lead you into greater insights. *Discovering John* is both an excellent group workbook and a personal workbook.

If you do not have a group to study with, you can still gain great benefit from using all the studies on your own. Simply adapt the group questions when needed.

If you are using this study book as a part of a Bible quizzing program, you will be getting the full benefit out of quizzing by doing so. But be careful! You will be tempted to slack off on your discovery workbook when you prepare for tournaments. Don't give in to that temptation! Gain the full benefit of memory work and application of biblical principles to your life as a disciple of Jesus Christ.

You are now invited to begin this special journey through John with Personal Discovery No. 1. Before you begin, pause for a moment of prayer, asking God to bless the time you give to the study of His Word, and to give you the desire to grow in your relationship with Him. And be prepared to make some exciting changes in your life!

SPECIAL INSTRUCTIONS: Each Personal Discovery is divided into five sections. All five can be done at once, but it will be more manageable—and probably more meaningful—if you do one section per day. In this way, the Personal Discoveries can be used as guides for your personal devotional times, as well as preparation for the Discovery Group sessions.

1 Why Jesus Became a Man

STUDY SCRIPTURE: John 1:1—2:11

KEY VERSE: "The Word became flesh and made his dwelling among us. We have seen his glory, the glory of the One and Only, who came from the Father, full of grace and truth" (John 1:14).

PERSONAL DISCOVERY

1. GETTING THE BIG PICTURE

For as long as anyone can remember, death has been beating up on the human race. We've tried a lot of things to stop the slaughter. First, we tried witch doctors and astrologers. Recently we've turned to medical doctors and philosophers, but it's all been pretty futile. Sure, we've learned to help people live a little longer, but ultimately, death always has its way.

The Gospel of John is an eyewitness account of the life and times of the only man in human history to have beaten death fair and square. By reading His story, you will learn His secret, and in the process, you will discover that His victory can be yours.

This study guide is intended to help you understand His story. It breaks the story down into 13 neat and manageable segments. Through the personal and group discovery process, you will gain a much deeper insight into the life of this remarkable Man.

Before you look at the parts, it's a good idea to look at the whole. Get acquainted with John's Gospel, by skimming through the 21 chapters. Try to answer the following questions.

▶ How many miracles are recorded in John's Gospel?

▶ If you divided the Gospel into two parts, where would you make the division and why?

▶ How many chapters describe the last night and day of Jesus' earthly life? Why is so much space given to just one day?

▶ In no more than 50 words, sum up what you believe to be the central message of the Gospel of John.

2. AGAINST THE GNOSTIC HERETICS! (1:1-18)

To understand the Gospel of John, you must understand the heresy of gnosticism. Heresies were spread by false teachers in the Early Church and came in many varieties. One of the more harmful heresies of early Christianity was gnosticism. Gnostics believed that matter was evil. Because of this conviction, gnostic teachers said that Jesus could not have had a real body; what people saw of Him was merely an image projected from heaven. (You know, kind of like a movie thrown onto a screen.) One of the purposes of John's Gospel is to set this whole crazy matter straight.

▶ Right in the first chapter John refutes gnostic thought. Which verses attack the gnostic notion that matter is evil?

Heresy? Don't I have the right to believe what I want to believe?

The Early Church fathers went to a great deal of trouble to help Christians understand who Jesus is and what God did for the world through Him. They labeled bad ideas and wrong teaching "heresy."

Heresy comes from the Greek word *hairein*, which means "to choose." Those who rejected the teaching of the early fathers were called "heretics" because they chose their own way rather than submit to the authority of the

Church. What's wrong with that? Aside from splitting the Church and confusing a lot of people, heresies, because they are the product of sloppy thinking, lead people into sin.

Gnosticism, one of the more common heresies then and now, leads to sins of irresponsibility. Here's how it happens. When people believe matter is evil, they abuse the environment, their communities and homes, and even their own bodies. They fail to act as stewards of creation because they don't see any connection between the physical world and God.

Like all heresies, gnosticism is a product of pride and laziness. It is overcome by humility and submission to the teaching of the Church.

▶ Why is gnosticism dangerous? Can you think of some ways gnosticism could lead to sin?

▶ The heresy of gnosticism is not merely a problem of the Early Church. Can you think of ways gnosticism has slipped into the Church today?

3. CAN I HEAR A WITNESS? (1:19-34)

How do you know what's true and what's false? You rely on authority and testimony. Here's an example. You probably believe the world is round. How do you know that? Did you actually go into outer space and take a look for yourself? No. You believed the testimony of people who have proven that the world is round.

But why do you trust these people? Maybe there's a big conspiracy; *maybe it's all a big joke!* Maybe your parents and teachers are laughing at you behind your back at this very minute! Nah, why should they go to all that trouble just to make you look dumb? You have no good reason not to believe them because they've told you the truth before. Why doubt them now? This is what is meant by authority and testimony. Sooner or later you've got to trust somebody.

▶ John the Baptist testifies that Jesus is the Christ, but why should we believe him?

► How does the Church witness to Jesus in the modern world?

► How can you witness for Jesus today?

4. AND THEY TELL TWO FRIENDS, AND SO ON! (1:35-51)

How did you first hear about Jesus? Was it by the testimony of someone you trust? In this passage we see a chain of testimonies and gain an understanding of how the disciples of Jesus multiplied.

► How did Andrew hear about Jesus?

► What did Andrew do when he believed?

► What did Philip do when he believed in Jesus?

► What do you think Jesus meant when He said to Nathanael, "You shall see heaven open, and the angels of God ascending and descending on the Son of Man" (v. 51)?

► Who witnessed to you about Jesus? Did you believe what they said? Why?

▶ Research indicates that over 90% of Christians believe in Jesus because of the witness of a friend, relative, or neighbor. This means we have more responsibility to witness to the people we know than to those we don't. Who do you know who needs to hear about Jesus?

5. SAVING THE BEST TILL LAST! (2:1-11)

This miracle is not about wine; it's about Jesus. It is a sign intended to make a point. That point is summed up by the master of the banquet, "Everyone brings out the choice wine first and then the cheaper wine after the guests have had too much to drink; but you have saved the best till now" (2:10). Jesus is the best that has been saved till last.

▶ Read chapter 1 verses 15 through 18. How do you understand the changing of the water to wine in light of this passage?

▶ In what ways is Jesus the best?

▶ What are some things people try before they taste Jesus?

DISCOVERY GROUP

STUDY SCRIPTURE: John 1:1—2:11

KEY VERSE: John 1:14

Mix and Match

Meet these citizens: Dr. Doom, Mr. Hedonist, and Ms. Faithful. Each read the Bible, attend church, and call themselves a Christian. What makes them different is their understanding of how Christians should relate to the world.

Dr. Doom and Mr. Hedonist have something in common; they both believe the world is evil. What makes them different is how they work out that conviction.

Dr. Doom is a morbid and kind of depressing person. He believes his bodily desires are evil, and is known for his long fasts. He believes that true spirituality begins with denying his flesh.

Mr. Hedonist, while of the same opinion says, "What's the use fighting it?" He believes the world is evil and his body is good for nothing, but since he's stuck with both he might as well enjoy them. Someone who watches Mr. Hedonist for a week might consider him a hypocrite. But it's not that he is dishonest, it's just that he lives in two worlds, a physical one and a spiritual one, and they don't always relate to each other.

Ms. Faithful believes that the creation is good because God made it. She also believes that her body is part of the creation. And she believes that, as a person made in God's image, she must care not only for her own body but for all of creation as well.

Based on their convictions, match the following statements with who you believe would say them. (DD—Dr. Doom, MH—Mr. Hedonist, or MF—for Ms. Faithful.)

____ "Hey, go ahead and abuse our parks. Jesus is coming back soon, and it's all gonna burn anyhow."

____ "It's a waste of time working to end hunger and suffering. It's a fallen world. What we should concentrate on is saving souls!"

____ "I'm so excited! Our teen group is going to work with Shepherd Community. I think we can make a real difference."

____ "You can't be honest and be a politician. That's why I don't vote for Christians. Morality gets in the way of getting things done in government! And besides, greed is good for the economy."

____ "Hey, how do you like my new Cadillac?"

___ "What does how I spend my free time have to do with God?"

___ "My blood pressure is high; I'm overweight; I eat greasy foods, smoke, stay up late, and in general enjoy myself. But what's the difference? We all die someday anyway."

Jesus and the World

In John 1:1, John calls Jesus "the Word." He then goes on to say in 1:3 that through Him all things were made. If we believe God is good, and we believe Jesus is good, then we must believe the creation is good. What are some practical implications of this? How should this conviction influence your attitudes toward . . .

- Personal health?

- Human suffering?

- The environment?

- Personal morality?

Caretakers of the World

Human beings are the caretakers of God's creation. Christians are called to witness, "This is my Father's world," and to keep it from being abused by selfish and sinful men. In what ways do people abuse God's good creation and how should Christians be different?

SINFUL ABUSE OF THE WORLD   **CHRISTIAN CARE OF THE WORLD**

How Can You Live More Responsibly?

Ask yourself these questions:

● If I truly believe that God created the world and then redeemed it through the presence of Jesus Christ, how should my life be different?

● What attitudes should I change and what beliefs should I repent of so that I can be a responsible Christian living in the world?

2 The Great Divide

STUDY SCRIPTURE: John 2:12—4:42

KEY VERSE: "Whoever believes in the Son has eternal life, but whoever rejects the Son will not see life, for God's wrath remains on him" (John 3:36).

PERSONAL DISCOVERY

1. OVERVIEW

Jews believed that they were God's favorite people. Consequently, they believed that they had a corner on the whole matter of salvation. They believed God's kingdom was a matter of being born in the right country, of worshiping in the right place, and having the right family background. Jesus demonstrates that salvation is for the whole world. In the process, He kills a few sacred cows. Read John 2:12—4:42 and see if you can spot some heifers.

▶ How do Jesus' actions in the Temple reveal God's displeasure with Jewish Temple worship?

▶ In chapter 3, Jesus sums up His mission in the world with a very familiar verse. What is it?

▶ In the second portion of chapter 3, John the Baptist sums up Jesus' mission in his own words. What does he say Jesus is here for?

> In chapter 4, a Samaritan woman asks Jesus where true worshipers meet. What does Jesus say?

2. THE NEW (AND IMPROVED) TEMPLE (2:12-25)

There's a reason the account of Jesus' actions at the Temple follow the miraculous sign at the wedding. As you can see in verse 12, some time passed between the incidents. But John places them back-to-back because the events interpret one another. If the message of the miracle at the wedding is that God has saved the best till last, then the message of the Temple incident is that Jesus is a better temple.

> Since Jesus is the Word made flesh, what do His actions at the Temple reveal concerning God's judgment upon Jewish Temple worship?

> When Jesus says He can raise the temple in three days, John is quick to tell us that He was referring to His body. Since the Jews understood the Temple to be the house of God (the residence of God's Spirit), what was the significance of Jesus calling His body a temple?

> Why is it important that Jesus predicted His death at the beginning of His ministry?

3. DIVIDING THE WORLD (3:1-36)

Jesus is perhaps the most controversial figure in human history. You either love Him or hate Him. Only the ignorant are neutral about Him. Jesus teaches Nicodemus that He has been sent into the world to save it. But personal salvation depends upon how He is received. God does not save people who would refuse His offer. Those who accept Him will be saved, but those who reject Him will be rejected.

▶ People are born into kingdoms, and since the Jews knew they were God's chosen people, it was logical to assume being born a Jew was the same thing as being born into God's kingdom. Not! Jesus shares with Nicodemus that birth into God's kingdom happens a whole different way. How?

▶ In verse 8, and again in verses 11-15, Jesus drops some hints about His origin and final destination. What are they?

▶ Why would Jesus' origin in God and ultimate destiny in God give His words more binding authority than the words of other men?

4. JESUS, THE SAVIOR OF THE WORLD (4:1-26)

After getting wind that the Pharisees are on His tail, Jesus detours north to Samaria, where He knows no self-respecting Pharisee will follow. But Jesus has more than escape on His mind; He is making a point. Remember, all of His actions communicate God's thoughts.

Samaritans were looked upon as half-breeds, part Jew and part Gentile. This made them worse than Gentiles in the minds of many Jews. By going among the Samaritans, Jesus communicated that God's love extends even to the Samaritans!

▶ Nothing recorded in the Gospels is without significance. If it's mentioned, it's important. The writer of John goes to great pains to tell us Jesus sat by Jacob's well. What's so important about that? (Hint: Jacob was the son of Isaac, who was the son of Abraham. God changed Jacob's name to Israel late in Jacob's life. In other words, the whole Jewish nation was descended from Jacob.)

▶ Jesus talks to a Samaritan woman at Jacob's well about water. By speaking of the water of Jacob's well, Jesus referred to the spiritual content of Jewish teaching. Then by speaking of himself as water, He spoke of the spiritual life that comes from hearing and obeying His words. Keeping in mind that Samaritans were considered outcasts from Israel, how did Jesus' words offer the woman new hope?

▶ Jesus' words concerning worship (vv. 21-24) should bring to mind the Temple incident from chapter 2. The Temple was located in Jerusalem, and Jews believed this was where the true worshipers of God gathered. Why is Jesus' teaching on worship good news for Samaritans and Gentiles?

5. HARVESTTIME (4:27-42)

One of the great Old Testament images for the "Day of Judgment" is harvesttime (Joel 3:13). This is the only mention of this image in the Gospel of John. The idea of harvest refers to the gathering of the righteous at the end of the world.

▶ Jesus tells His disciples to open their eyes and see the fields all around them (v. 35). Which fields do you suppose He was referring to?

▶ Summarize, in your own words, how Jesus' actions in chapters 2—4 demonstrate that God's salvation is for all the world.

DISCOVERY GROUP

STUDY SCRIPTURE: John 2:12—4:42

KEY VERSE: John 3:36

What Needs Healing?

Salvation is a big word. Nine letters is not what makes it big, though. Its meaning is what makes it big. Salvation has the same Latin root as the word *salve*. Salve is a healing ointment. Salvation is the healing ointment of God. It is intended to heal everything that needs healing. It heals our broken relationship with our Creator, and from there, all other relationships. Let's look at what needs healing in our world. Starting with you, what needs healing in your life? What needs healing in:

- Your home?

- Your school?

- Your church?

- Your city?

- Your nation?

- Your world?

The Light of the World

In John's Gospel, eternal life and salvation are two ways of saying the same thing. In John 3:17 it says, "God did not send his Son into the world to condemn the world, but to save the world through him." The question remains, how does Jesus bring God's healing power into our world? Read John 3:16-21 and answer the following questions:

1. What are the qualities of light that humans need?

2. Why do some people stay in the dark?

3. Why do others choose to enter into the light?

Now read 1 John 1:5-10:

4. According to verse 7, what happens when people walk in the light?

5. How does verse 9 help clarify the meaning of walking in the light?

6. How does light heal the world?

Leaving the Darkness Behind

Taking our medicine can be painful, but healing is worth the pain. But not everyone believes this. Jesus says in John 3:19, "This is the verdict: Light has come into the world, but men loved darkness instead of light because their deeds were evil." Jesus can't help people who won't step into the light of truth.

What would you say to a friend who remains in the darkness of denial? How will you attempt to convince that person that living in the light is better?

A Prayer of Healing

We can't force people to confess their sins, but we can pray for them. In this lesson we have seen how Jesus has judged the world. Those who speak the truth and confess their sins, He heals. But those who hide in the darkness stand condemned. Pray for yourself. Then pray for your family, your church, your school, your nation, your city, and the world. Pray that we all become willing to be healed in the light of Jesus Christ.

3 Working with God

STUDY SCRIPTURE: John 4:43—5:47

KEY VERSE: "Jesus said to them, 'My Father is always at his work to this very day, and I, too, am working'" (John 5:17).

PERSONAL DISCOVERY

1. OVERVIEW

The story begins with the incredible account of the Incarnation; Jesus, the Word of God, comes into the world to reveal the Father to helpless humanity. After He calls His first disciples and performs His first miraculous sign, Jesus confronts the corrupt Jewish leaders at the Temple, the center of Jewish life. Here He predicts His death at their hands and His resurrection from the dead by the power of God. After this, during a late night rendezvous, Jesus tells Nicodemus, a member of the Sanhedrin, that entrance into the kingdom of God is a matter of spiritual birth, not physical birth. Then, upon hearing that the Pharisees are after Him, Jesus heads to Samaria, where He demonstrates the universal dimensions of salvation by extending it to the hated Samaritans.

Now Jesus is back in Jerusalem for another confrontation with the Jewish leadership. The hearts and minds of the people are at stake. Jesus attacks the religious status quo by defying official teaching and healing a man on the Sabbath. Those who witness the healing are forced to judge who speaks for God: the Jewish authorities or the maverick Teacher from Galilee.

Read the assigned scripture for this session, and answer the following questions.

▶ What do you think Jesus' attitude toward performing miracles was?

▶ Is there anything Jesus says or does that surprises you? Why?

▶ Write down three key thoughts regarding the Sabbath.

2. HEALING THE ROYAL OFFICIAL'S SON (4:43-54)

People in all places and at all times long for miracles. In one sense, this is a good thing. It indicates that people have a need to encounter the Divine. On the other hand, this longing can go downhill quickly. It can be like people asking God to pull a rabbit out of a hat to the applause of the crowd.

Here we see Jesus putting miracles into perspective. He says, "Unless you people see miraculous signs and wonders, you will never believe" (v. 48). Then He proceeds to provide a miraculous sign. The message is fairly straightforward: signs help us believe, but it is better if we can believe without them.

▶ Jesus calls His miracles "signs." Signs point to something; they are not an end in themselves. What are the signs of Jesus intended to show us?

▶ Did the royal official's faith begin when he took Jesus at His word—or later when he heard news of the healing?

▶ Should people expect to see miracles every day, or has the age of miracles come to an end? Or, is the truth somewhere in the middle?

▶ Have you ever seen a miracle? If so, what did you learn from it?

3. HEALING ON THE SABBATH (5:1-15)

Before hospitals and the advent of modern medicine, the sick and disabled, desperate for any hope of healing, would try just about anything. Occasionally, a tale or a legend would develop about this or that cure, and before you knew it, a stampede of sick people gathered to be healed. This was the case at the pool of Bethesda. According to legend, periodically an angel descended from heaven and stirred healing power into the waters of the pool. The first one in was to be healed. This is why so many sick people were hanging out by the pool. (In other words, it wasn't to get a tan.)

Only two healings recorded in the Gospel of John were initiated by Jesus—this one, and the healing of a blind man in chapter 9. Both of these occurred on the Sabbath. It's hard to imagine that a healing could be scandalous, but both of these healings were. According to Jewish law, no work was to be done on the Sabbath, and Jesus, being a good Jew, knew this. But He healed anyway.

▶ If Jesus knew what the Jewish leadership would say about healing on the Sabbath, why did He do it?

▶ Jesus commands the lame man to "pick up your mat and walk" (v. 8). He knew this would advertise the healing. Why didn't He just heal the guy quietly and keep it a secret between friends?

▶ It is not uncommon for religious people to get caught up in rules. The Jewish leaders, in their zeal to keep the Sabbath, forgot why it was instituted in the first place. Can you think of ways Christians are at times guilty of the same thing?

The Plot Is Hatched!

"For this reason the Jews tried all the harder to kill him" (v. 18).

From the beginning of Jesus' ministry, forces were at work to kill Him. While this is not the first hint that Jesus will die, it is the first time we see the Jews at work to kill Him. Their intentions certainly did not catch Jesus by surprise. He understood the minds of men and knew what they were capable of. As early as chapter 2, Jesus foretold that He would die at the hands of the Jews.

From this point on keep your eyes open for the unfolding conspiracy to kill Jesus. As you read, try to imagine what "life on the run" was like for Jesus, and attempt to understand why the Jews sought to kill Him. And finally, look for how Jesus used this very thing, His own murder, to glorify His Father.

4. WORK (5:16-30)

By healing on the Sabbath, Jesus created a crisis among the people. He defied the authority of the Jewish leaders and declared that He was God's authoritative Spokesman. It's understandable why the Jewish leaders didn't like this idea (regardless of the miracle). It was a clear threat to their position. But this was the point: Jesus wanted the people to choose between himself and the Jewish leaders. He wanted the people to believe in Him so that they might have life through Him.

▶ How does Jesus defend the healing in verses 17-20? What is the gist of His argument?

▶ The fourth of the Ten Commandments requires Jews to keep the Sabbath day and do no work on it. (Check it out in Exodus 20:8-11 and Deuteronomy 5:12-15.) In their practice of this commandment, the Jews missed the point somewhere. Where do you believe they went wrong?

▶ In verse 20, Jesus says, "For the Father loves the Son and shows him all he does. Yes, to your amazement he will show him even greater things than these." He then goes on to explain what He means by "greater things" in verses 21-30. What are the greater things?

▶ Throughout His discourse, Jesus again and again says that the authority He exercises is not His own. Whose authority is it, and how does He prove it?

▶ This section has shown us God at work. Based upon what you have read, what is the nature of God's work?

5. TESTIMONY (5:31-47)

In verses 31-47, Jesus makes some pretty bold claims for himself. Someone once said that either Jesus was an egomaniac, or He was who He claimed to be. For the people who heard His claims, believing in Jesus meant rejecting the Jewish leadership and following Him. Things haven't changed. Today believing in Him means rejecting the world and making Him the authoritative Center of our life.

▶ Read through the scripture and list the sources of testimony Jesus appeals to.

▶ Jesus gives reasons why the Jewish leaders reject this testimony. List the reasons here.

▶ In verses 41-44, Jesus says that those who accept praise from men but do not seek praise from God will never believe in Him. Can you think of some examples of people you know who do not believe in Jesus because they are more concerned about the opinion of people?

▶ Why do you believe in Jesus? What testimony did you hear that helped faith develop in your life?

DISCOVERY GROUP

STUDY SCRIPTURE: John 4:43—5:47

KEY VERSE: John 5:17

Flipping Burgers

More teens have jobs these days than ever before. When I say that, I don't mean other generations of teens were lazy. In fact, they may have worked longer and harder than teens do these days. In the old days, life on the farm began early each day. Teens were expected to put in a couple of hours doing chores before school, and a few more when they got home after school. What I mean by jobs today is employment outside the home. Most teens today work just for money. They probably don't work at McDonald's flipping burgers because they believe flipping burgers makes the world a better place. They flip burgers because they're paid to flip burgers.

But Christians never do anything just for money. We work to glorify God and serve His world. Right? Below is a list of jobs teens usually do for money. Think of how each of these jobs can be understood to glorify God and serve His creation.

The Job	*The Christian Purpose*
1. Flipping Burgers at McDonald's	
2. Baby-sitting/Day Care	
3. Mowing Lawns	
4. Waitress/Waiter	
5. Clerk in a Supermarket	
6. Other (your job if not listed)	

God's Résumé

God is a "workingman's" God. When we read the Bible, we see Him getting down on His hands and knees and getting His hands into the need of the world.

For the purposes of this exercise, imagine God is looking for work, and He needs to write a résumé. Use Genesis 1:1—2:3 and John 3:2—5:47 to provide some background on what God has done and what He is qualified to do. Use the following outline to guide you in writing God's résumé.

Name: God

Address: Heaven

Objective: (What kind of employment is God looking for?)

Experience: (What has He done that qualifies Him for such employment?)

Awards and Honors:

References:

Personal Data:

Birth Date:

Working with God

When you become a Christian, you join the "God Squad." That means you work because God works, and you rest because He rests. Jesus shows us what it means to work with God. It means we do what we see God doing. And how do we know what God is doing? By looking at Jesus.

As Christians, we believe God created the world. This means that there is no job that cannot be understood as a working-with-God job. (Except, of course, work that is blatantly sinful like prostitution, and, therefore, is not true work at all.) Martin Luther is reported to have said that a man can glorify God just as well by plowing a field as by singing "Hallelujah!" in church. What makes a job a "God job" is working to glorify God and serve His creation.

Imagine you have dreams and hopes for your vocation in life. You may want to be a businessperson, a lawyer, an engineer, a pilot, or a homemaker (needed now more than ever—we have an actual shortage of real homes in our world!). Think of something you would like to do, and think about it as a "God job." How can it be done in a way that glorifies God and serves His creation?

Take a Break!

The proverb says, "All work and no play makes Jack a dull boy." While God is a working God, He is also a God of rest. In the creation He established a pattern of work and rest in which rest follows work as a time of celebration. Rest reflects on work and prepares those who labor to work again. It is a time of joy.

Once upon a time in many countries, it was illegal to work on Sunday. Everyone was forced to take the day off. Sadly, we've lost a common day of rest. In the space below, record why rest is good and important for Christians, and reflect on why a common day of rest is a good thing for everybody.

4 The Bread and the Blood

STUDY SCRIPTURE: John 6:1-71

KEY VERSE: Jesus said to them, "I tell you the truth, unless you eat the flesh of the Son of Man and drink his blood, you have no life in you" (John 6:53).

PERSONAL DISCOVERY

1. OVERVIEW

Jesus has set the forces in motion that will ultimately carry Him to His death. His destiny upon the Cross has been alluded to twice, once by Jesus himself in the Temple (2:19), and again by the writer of this Gospel (5:18). But now we've turned a corner in the narrative. From this point on, Jesus gives repeated attention to His impending death. As strange as it may sound, the feeding of the 5,000 and the walk on the water are both signs that point to the Cross. They are symbols that help us make sense of His death and give us a way of understanding how it can change our lives.

▶ With the death of Jesus in mind, read these stories and the teaching that follows. Can you see anything in them that might point to Jesus and His death upon the Cross?

▶ Is there anything in the scripture that you find interesting or shocking?

▶ Does anything remind you of Communion?

▶ Does anything remind you of baptism?

2. FEEDING THE 5,000 (6:1-15)

Nearly a year has passed since Jesus cleansed the Temple. He is now in Galilee, teaching huge crowds that have begun to follow Him. Since the Feast of Passover is near, Jesus asks His disciples to get some food for the crowd. They are completely dumbfounded. What happens next is one of the best-known and least-understood miracles recorded in the Bible. Jesus feeds 5,000 people with five loaves and two fish.

Since we will not fully understand the meaning of the miracle until later, let's spend some time highlighting and exploring some of the features of the story.

▶ The time is the Passover. This is an important clue to understanding everything that follows. Passover was a time to remember the slaying of the Egyptian firstborn. You can read in Exodus about how God sent an angel of death to slay all the firstborn in the land of Egypt. But the Hebrews were exempt if they smeared the blood of a lamb on the doorposts of their homes. That's how the death angel knew to pass over their homes. (Hence the name "Passover.") Christians call Jesus "the Lamb of God." How does the sacrifice of a Passover lamb point to the sacrifice of Jesus?

▶ Numbers are important in the Bible. They're full of symbolic significance. List some of the numbers recorded in John 6:1-15. Any ideas on what the numbers might symbolize?

▶ Verses 13 and 14 show that a significant portion of food was left over. Can you think of any symbolic reasons that this was so?

3. A STROLL ON THE LAKE (6:16-24)

Here is another well-known and greatly misunderstood miracle story. Remember, Jesus' miracles were signs that served to illuminate His mission in the world.

▶ There is a number recorded in this story. What is it, and what does it remind you of?

▶ What Christian sacrament involves water? How is this story similar to that sacrament?

▶ Can you see any significance in the disciples leaving the crowd on the opposite side of the lake?

4. THE BREAD OF LIFE (6:25-59)

Now that we've looked at the signs, Jesus helps us make sense of them. Jesus refers to himself as "the bread of God" and "the bread of Life." When Jesus gave the bread to the crowd, He was in fact giving himself to the crowd. This is why there was more than enough to go around, for Jesus will die for the whole world. And perhaps this is why 12 basketfuls remain; there is a basket for each apostle to distribute to the world. And this all happened at Passover because Jesus is the Lamb of God whose blood shields those who believe in Him from the angel of death.

The theme is further developed by two related word pictures. First, since people work for "bread," Jesus calls His listeners to work for the bread He gives. (Of course, the crowd really wants a free lunch like their ancestors in the wilderness got. They want manna.)

▶ In verse 27, what does Jesus say is the work that earns eternal life?

▶ Jesus constructs an elaborate parallel between himself and manna; how is He like it?

▶ Verses 37 and 44 seem to indicate that receiving the bread of life is not wholly our choice. Whose decision is it?

▶ Jesus' language in verses 51-58 is very graphic. The Jews take offense and ask, "How can this man give us his flesh to eat?" How would you answer that question?

▶ Verse 41 says that the Jews began to grumble about Jesus because He said, "I am the bread that came down from heaven." Can you think of another time when Jews grumbled about heavenly bread?

Manna—What Is It?

In case you're wondering what this manna business is all about, read Exodus 16. Manna was a breadlike substance that fell from the sky while the Israelites wandered in the wilderness after escaping Egypt. Each morning they gathered just enough for that day, believing that God would provide enough again the next day.

Since manna had never been seen before (or since), it was an oddity. When the Jews first saw it, they exclaimed, *"Manna?"* which is Hebrew for "What is it?" The name stuck.

5. THE DISCIPLES DESERT JESUS (6:60-71)

While the previous teaching section helped illuminate the meaning of the feeding of the 5,000, this section helps us understand the meaning of the walk on the water. The key is understanding that water symbolizes death. Early Christians used the sign of a fish for Christ, because He went beneath the surface of the earth for three days, as Jonah went beneath water for three days. The whole event is a code that points us to the death of Jesus and its significance for His disciples.

When we are baptized, we identify with Jesus by going beneath the surface of the water and dying to sin. We confess our faith in His resurrection by being lifted from the water. It is by this identification that we are separated from the world and leave the crowd on the opposite shore.

▶ According to verse 60, what did many of the disciples do upon hearing Jesus' teaching?

▶ What does Peter say on behalf of the Twelve to express their commitment to Jesus?

DISCOVERY GROUP

STUDY SCRIPTURE: John 6:1-71

KEY VERSE: John 6:53

Living on Death

This may be a morbid thing to do, but think about a visit to the supermarket—and imagine the store is filled with dead stuff. Go to the meat department, and when you see the drumsticks, say to yourself, "Dead chicken legs." When you go to the vegetable department, look at the ears of corn, and say to yourself, "The dead seeds of a dead cornstalk." As you go through the store, look for stuff to eat that isn't dead, and make a list. Your list will be very short. In fact, it will be blank because our bodies live on the death of other once-living things.

How is what is true for the body true for the spirit?

The Great Communion Debate

Jesus gave His body as a sacrifice so that we might eat His flesh and drink His blood and live. These are Jesus' own words. But the big question is, how do we do it?

Over time, three understandings have emerged that help Christians understand the relationship between Communion and the spiritual life we receive from Jesus. (They're expressed in big words, so get ready!)

1. Transubstantiation

This belief holds that when Christians celebrate the Lord's Supper, the "substance" beneath the appearance of the bread and wine miraculously transforms into the body and blood of Jesus. In this tradition the elements are called the "host" because they carry the very body and blood of Jesus. While the appearance of the elements is still the same, they actually are the body and blood of Jesus.

2. Consubstantiation

While this view sounds a lot like transubstantiation, it is different. "Con" means "with." These Christians believe the *spiritual* body and blood of Jesus is "with" the elements. Again, the bread and wine look like bread and wine, but Jesus is within the elements. It's more than bread and wine—it is bread and wine plus Jesus.

3. Symbolic

This view is very different from those above. Christians with this view celebrate Communion, but for them, the bread is just bread and the wine is just wine. It is a memorial. The power of the celebration is the reminder it provides of God's grace in Christ. In this view, Jesus is received by the power of the Holy Spirit without the aid of a sacrament. Nonetheless, Jesus is present in the celebration, because Jesus is always present when believers gather in His name.

As you can imagine, these views affect how Christians celebrate Communion. Try to label different attitudes below with the theory listed above: 1 for transubstantiation; 2 for consubstantiation; and 3 for symbolic.

1. _____ Father Flannigan said to us in the hospital emergency room, "I'm glad I got here when I did; I was able to give him the body and blood of Jesus before he died."

2. _____ "I've got to get to Church. I haven't had Communion in over a week!"

3. _____ Pastor Johnson said, "Phil, could you run down to the store and pick up some Wonder bread and grape juice? We're celebrating the Lord's Supper in the evening service."

4. _____ "We have Communion at our church about once every three months."

5. _____ "The high point of every service at our church is the celebration of Holy Communion."

Which view, if any, have you been taught? Which seems most honest to you? What do you think Communion really is?

Celebrating Communion

Why is it important for Christians to faithfully receive the Lord's Supper?

What has your attitude been?

When taking Communion, have you really recognized all that Jesus Christ has done?

5 What Will You Choose?

STUDY SCRIPTURE: John 7:1—8:30

KEY VERSE: "If anyone chooses to do God's will, he will find out whether my teaching comes from God or whether I speak on my own" (John 7:17).

PERSONAL DISCOVERY

1. OVERVIEW

Like a great knife, Jesus has descended from heaven to divide the Jewish nation. By cleansing the Temple and healing a man on the Sabbath, He exposed the fraud of the religious leaders. Because He exercised authority and power independent of, and in direct conflict with, the authorities, He demonstrated that God was with Him. For this He has become a fugitive on the run.

Now we see that the tension continues to build between Jesus and the Jewish leadership. Jesus knows that He is hated by His enemies and celebrated by those who believe in Him. And He even encourages this division, for by it, God is judging the nation and revealing the hearts of people.

▶ Read the Scripture passage and circle the word below that you believe best describes the mood of the passage.

> joy   conflict   peace   anger   salvation

▶ Sum up the message Jesus presents to the Jews in a couple of sentences.

▶ If you have ever confronted a corrupt system of power, you know it takes enormous courage and determination to face it. Where did Jesus find the strength to do what He did?

▶ Have you ever found yourself in a situation where speaking truth made you very unpopular? If so, describe it and the lessons you learned by it.

2. THE WORLD HATES ME (7:1-13)

When Jesus said, "The world . . . hates me," He wasn't giving himself a pity party. He was stating a fact. He had plenty of reason to believe as He did—after all, the Jews were trying to kill Him.

▶ Verse 5 shows us that even His own brothers did not believe in Him. Have you ever found yourself in the same position—despised for your faith in God and mocked by the members of your own family? How do you handle it?

▶ In verse 7 Jesus reveals why the world hates Him. Why do people hate to have their evil deeds exposed?

▶ Jesus secretly goes to the feast and overhears the opinions of the people concerning Him. Some like Him but some definitely do not. Why?

3. THE MAN OF TRUTH (7:14-24)

Jesus reveals himself at the feast and teaches openly. The crowd is astonished at His teaching because He was not trained at one of the rabbinical schools of the day. Jesus uses their astonishment to point out that His teaching is not from men, but from God. Then He provides a test to verify the truthfulness of

His claims. In verse 17 He declares, "If anyone chooses to do God's will, he will find out whether my teaching comes from God or whether I speak on my own."

▶ This means those who do not choose God's will cannot see the Source of Jesus' teaching. Sin blinds their inner eye. When people fail to see the truth in Jesus, how can we help open their eyes?

▶ As we see in chapter 7, speaking the truth often makes one extremely unpopular. How about you? Are you prepared to follow the Man of truth—even if accepting His message means being hated by the world?

▶ Something is not necessarily truth simply because the majority believe it is. Jesus shows us that truth has nothing to do with popularity contests. Truth is truth whether or not it is honored by the majority. Where do Christians find the strength to do what is right when the whole world is against it?

4. JESUS DIVIDES THE PEOPLE (7:25-52)

Here we see Jesus, the Man of truth, separating those who do God's will from those who do not. The people judge themselves by their judgment of Jesus. Some believe Him, while others reject Him. And Jesus allows their judgments to stand—against themselves.

▶ In verses 25-27 and 41-42, the Jews wonder how Jesus can be the Christ when He comes from Galilee. What is Jesus' response in verses 28 and 29?

▶ When the chief priests and Pharisees sent Temple guards to arrest Him, Jesus explained, "I am with you for only a short time, and then I [will] go to the one who sent me." What did the Jews think He meant by this? What do you think He meant?

▶ On the first day of the feast, Jesus promised a blessing for those who believe in Him. What was the blessing?

▶ Verses 30 and 44 say that the Jews tried to arrest Jesus, but that they couldn't lay a hand on Him "because his time had not yet come." When the Temple guards reported their failure to the priests in verses 45 and 46, the Pharisees declare, "Has any of the rulers or [any] of the Pharisees believed in him?" Well, did any? (Look at verses 50-51.)

5. JESUS' TESTIMONY (8:12-30)

Jesus tells the Jews that since He knows where He comes from and where He is going, and since they haven't got a clue, He is the Light, and they are still in the darkness of their sins. But a time is coming when they will see "the Son of Man . . . lifted up" (v. 28), and they will know who He is.

▶ What time is Jesus referring to? And how will people finally recognize who He is?

Lifted Up

"When you have lifted up the Son of Man . . ."

This is not the first or the last time we will hear Jesus say this. The first time was "Just as Moses lifted up the snake in the desert, so the Son of Man must be lifted up, that everyone who believes in him may have eternal life" (3:14-15).

The phrase "lifted up" was intended to bring to mind the story of Moses and the bronze snake (Numbers 21:4-9). Once, when the Israelites were plagued by snakes during their wilderness trek, Moses was instructed by God to make a bronze snake and place it on a pole so that the poisoned might look upon it and live. Jesus declares that He is like the bronze snake, and when He is lifted up, those who look upon Him and believe will have eternal life.

DISCOVERY GROUP

STUDY SCRIPTURE: John 7:1—8:30

KEY VERSE: John 7:17

Speaking Up

John hated going to class. Contemporary Social Issues was an interesting class. He didn't hate it because it was boring. He hated how Ms. Clark taught it. Instead of a balanced presentation of social issues, the class was a time for Ms. Clark to make her points to the applause and boisterous laughter of the class. Name the issue, and Ms. Clark advocated a perspective John disagreed with: homosexuality, abortion, family issues, whatever. In each case the traditional way of doing things was "oppressive," and letting people do whatever they pleased was "liberating."

Her favorite target for mockery was Christians, particularly television preachers who she would mimic for the class. According to Ms. Clark, all Christians were uptight, intellectual Neanderthals who wanted to return to the Dark Ages.

Everyone seemed to enjoy her tirades with the exception of John. He was the only Christian in the class. Occasionally he would raise his hand to make an objection, but each time he chickened out. What's the use? he thought.

Today's class was going to be particularly difficult. The subject for discussion was the "Rights of Homosexuals to Adopt Children." The night before, John had been in a revival service at his church. The preacher was good and had spoken on "taking a stand for Jesus." John knew what that meant for him. He had to speak up in Contemporary Social Issues.

John found his seat, and Ms. Clark began her show. She spoke movingly of how homosexuals have been persecuted and tortured throughout history and why they should be accepted as "just ordinary people with different tastes." Then she began with the jokes, mocking Christian morality. John looked around the room and saw the faces of his friends contorted with laughter. John's heart was racing and his palms were sweaty as he said to himself, "It's now or never." Slowly he raised his trembling hand.

- Have you ever found yourself in a situation like John's?

Accountability

It will take a lot of courage for John to speak the truth in Contemporary Social Issues. But he must, because if he doesn't, he will deny who he is and what he believes. Beyond that, Ms. Clark and the students in the class will have no one to hold them accountable. And according to Scripture, when someone knows God's Word but refuses to speak it, God holds them accountable for the sins of the wicked.

"When I say to a wicked man, 'You will surely die,' and you do not warn him or speak out to dissuade him from his evil ways in order to save his life, that wicked man will die for his sin, and I will hold you accountable for his blood" (Ezekiel 3:18).

- On what issues should Christians take a stand?

- What's the most effective way to communicate to non-Christians?

Jesus' Example

Jesus knew what it was like to take a stand for truth. He doesn't expect us to do anything He didn't do himself. And because we are His followers, we must follow His example. The following scriptures will help you see how Jesus understood the difficulty of speaking the truth. What do you learn from each one?

1. Why do people hate Jesus? (7:1-13)

2. How can people know the truth? (7:16-17)

3. Jesus teaches that people speak for two reasons. What are they? (7:16-29)

A Covenant of Truth

Jesus spoke the truth, even though it made Him unpopular and ultimately got Him killed by evil men. He did this because He loved us and wanted us to know the truth. Because He did this for us, we also ought to do this for Him and for those who have not yet believed. In the space below, write out a promise to Jesus that you will follow His example.

6 True or False?

STUDY SCRIPTURE: John 8:31—9:41

KEY VERSE: "If you hold to my teaching, you are really my disciples. Then you will know the truth, and the truth will set you free" (John 8:31-32).

PERSONAL DISCOVERY

1. OVERVIEW

The Man from above has brought the Word of God below and has judged the world by seeking to save it. To those who believe in Him He gives eternal life, but those who reject Him stand condemned. In this session, we see Jesus in the heat of a debate, debunking the Jewish self-understanding that they were the stewards of God's Word. First, He tells them they are slaves; then He calls them illegitimate children. Later, He says they have no spiritual understanding; but worst of all, He shows them that they serve the devil and not the one true God.

▶ Read the Study Scripture and describe the mood Jesus appears to be in.

▶ Why do you suppose Jesus was so committed to undermining the authority of the Jewish religious leadership?

▶ Considering the many miracles Jesus performed and the power of His teaching, why didn't the Jewish leaders accept Jesus as who He claimed to be?

2. YOU'RE NOT FREE (John 8:31-34)

When I was a teen, I had no understanding of freedom. I thought it meant doing whatever I wanted to do. Only later I came to understand that it is possible to be a slave to your passions. I didn't know that passions are not what make persons who they are. True freedom is the freedom to do what is right.

▶ In verses 31 and 32, Jesus provides a potent formula for freedom; what is it?

▶ The Jews believed freedom was a matter of genetics. Since they were descendants of a free man, they believed they were free. Describe Jesus' response in verse 34.

▶ How does holding to Jesus' teachings make us free? In other words, by following Jesus how are we made free?

3. YOU'RE NOT ABRAHAM'S CHILDREN (8:35-40)

It seems odd today that the Jews should appeal to Abraham as proof of their freedom. But Jesus didn't think it was odd; He just didn't think it was true. Slavery was often a family affair in ancient times; slaves produced slaves. So Jews, never mind their slavery in Egypt, counted themselves free men. But Jesus was not talking about physical slavery; He was speaking of spiritual slavery.

Physical children resemble their parents, and so do spiritual children. And with this argument, Jesus refutes the Jews' identification with Abraham (vv. 39 and 40). Abraham obeyed God, but they don't. That makes them slaves, not sons.

▶ While Jesus' words are harsh, they are not cruel. Even as He condemns them, He holds out hope for the Jews. What is the hope Jesus holds out to them?

▶ Jesus tells the Jews that their plans to kill Him prove what?

▶ So why are the Jews trying to kill Jesus?

4. YOU'RE CHILDREN OF THE DEVIL (8:41-59)

So who do the Jews resemble? Jesus confronts them with their actions: they reject truth and attempt murder. These actions certainly don't appear to be god-like. Whose behavior do they resemble?

▶ In verse 47, Jesus declares, "He who belongs to God hears what God says." And the reverse of that must also be true: "He who belongs to the devil . . ." Finish the sentence.

▶ What does Jesus say that hints that He is one with the Father?

▶ What do verses 37, 40, 43, and 45 have in common?

5. YOU CAN'T SEE (9:1-41)

This is the sixth of the seven miraculous signs of Jesus recorded in John's Gospel. But while it is the sixth, it also seems to be a repeat of miracle number three, the healing of the lame man on the Sabbath back in chapter 5. While the similarity is strong, and many issues are the same, the primary purpose of the story is to seal Jesus' case against the Jewish leadership and demonstrate why they are unfit to lead the people of God.

▶ Read the whole story and write down every verse that alludes to sight, seeing, or perceiving.

▶ The investigation of the healing provides some good fun at the expense of the Pharisees. In what way does the investigation prove the Pharisees are blind?

▶ Why would this kind of blindness disqualify someone from spiritual leadership?

▶ Considering Jesus' words in verses 39 and 41, what is the key to spiritual sight?

DISCOVERY GROUP

STUDY SCRIPTURE: John 8:31—9:41

KEY VERSE: John 8:31-32

The Age of Martyrs Is Not Over

If you read the New Testament, you know that the early Christians suffered for their faith in Jesus. Both Peter and Paul died because of their preaching. For the next 250 years, Christians were persecuted throughout the Roman empire.

The age of martyrs is not over. It is believed that more Christians have died for speaking the truth in the 20th century than in all 19 previous centuries combined. While some have died here in North America and in Europe, most of the killing has occurred in Africa, Latin America, and Asia.

- Why do evil people and systems hate the truth so much?

- Can you think of examples of how evil seeks to suppress truth?

- How would you respond if you were not allowed to follow the truth?

Light or Dark?

In the Scriptures, light is God's truth and darkness is man's sinfulness. Light and life go together, since God is the Author of both, and He cannot be divided against himself. This means sin, falsehood, and death all belong together, for they are not from God. Mark whether you believe each of the following deeds belongs to darkness (D) or light (L).

____ 1. Caring for the poor

____ 2. Speaking negatively about people who aren't present

___ 3. Speaking the truth

___ 4. Loving your neighbor

___ 5. Telling ethnic jokes

___ 6. Refusing to slander a person's character

___ 7. Wasting money on selfish purchases

___ 8. Reaching out across ethnic and racial barriers

___ 9. Killing people

___ 10. Stealing

___ 11. Honesty in all your ways

___ 12. Homosexual relationships

___ 13. Abusing your body through various toxic substances

___ 14. Cheating on taxes

___ 15. Honoring your parents

___ 16. Caring for God's creation

___ 17. Identifying with the outcast

Finding Help to Tell the Truth

It takes great strength and courage to do what is right because it is so easy to do what is wrong. In order to do what is right, you need help. You're too weak to do it on your own. We all need this kind of support. That's why Christian friends, people who believe Jesus is the Way, the Truth, and the Life, are so important. Who are your friends? Who are the people who support you and help you do what is right? (If you don't have such friends, you need to find them quick!) Who do you know that lives the Christian life and can help you to as well?

● List the friends who help you live like a Christian.

● How do they support you?

● Do you have friends who tend to lower your standards and practice?

Giving Help

Not only do you need help to tell the truth, but also others need your help. In this space write out prayers for the following people.

Christian friends

Leaders in your church

Christian leaders in our nation

Christians around the world who are daring to speak the truth

7 **The Good Shepherd**

STUDY SCRIPTURE: John 10:1-42

KEY VERSE: "I am the good shepherd. The good shepherd lays down his life for the sheep" (John 10:11).

PERSONAL DISCOVERY

1. OVERVIEW

Jesus' public ministry is nearly at an end. He came to bring salvation, but the Jews have condemned themselves by condemning Him. In the last session we witnessed Jesus' judgment of the Jewish religious authorities as He systematically refuted their self-understanding that they are the stewards of God's Word.

In chapter 10, Jesus illustrates His salvation through the imagery of a shepherd and his sheep. The Jewish golden era was ushered in by a shepherd named David. The Jews longed for another David who would "restore the kingdom to Israel" (Acts 1:6). But the kind of shepherd Jesus describes is not the shepherd they've been waiting for.

▶ Read chapter 10 and jot down some of your images of the Good Shepherd. (Is He really like the happy paintings used in junior church or is He something more?)

▶ As you read about the Good Shepherd, how does the imagery help you understand what has happened up to this point in John's Gospel?

▶ The image of the Good Shepherd also points toward some events that have yet to occur. Can you think of some?

2. VOICES (John 10:1-8)

Jesus begins with an image that must have been familiar to His listeners. In those days, cities were much closer to farms than they usually are today. Everyone knew about shepherds because they were a common sight. It was also common for teachers to use the shepherd and his work as a metaphor for religious instruction. While the imagery was just as warm and comforting for the Jews as it is for us, it held a greater power for them because of their hope of a shepherd king, who, like David, would establish God's kingdom on the earth.

Jesus' story contains a hint of judgment for the sheep that is entirely new. The popular vision celebrated happy sheep and doom for wolves. This rendering describes a selective shepherd and a feast for wolves.

▶ Jesus explains that He has come to the sheep pen of Israel and has called out the names of His sheep. What is the one thing that separates Jesus' sheep from the sheep who do not belong to Him?

▶ Jesus describes those who came before Him as "thieves and robbers" (v. 8). Who do you think He was speaking of?

▶ Jesus says His sheep do not listen to a stranger's voice. How do the sheep tell the difference between the voice of the Good Shepherd and other voices?

3. THE GOOD SHEPHERD (John 10:9-15)

The difference between the Good Shepherd and the hired hands is the sacrifice the shepherd makes for the sheep. When the wolf comes, hired hands drop their staffs, run, and leave the sheep as easy meat. But the Good Shepherd gives His own life that the sheep may live.

▶ When Jesus speaks of the Good Shepherd, He is speaking of himself (v. 11), but who are the hired hands?

▶ Jesus speaks of a wolf who is coming. It is not a matter of *if*, but *when*. Jesus is removing His sheep from the pen and leaving those who are not His own to the care of the hired hands. And as we see from verses 12 and 13, it looks like they will be meat for the wolf. Why is Jesus leaving them behind?

▶ Jumping ahead to verse 17, Jesus says the reason the Father loves the Son is because He gives His life for the sheep. This is why the Father has taken His sheep from the hired hands and given them to the Good Shepherd. When Jesus speaks of laying down His life for the sheep, what is He talking about?

▶ Why do hired hands work with sheep?

▶ We call spiritual leaders "pastors" because they are supposed to be like Jesus, the Good Shepherd. Use this passage of Scripture as a guide, and write a job description for a pastor.

4. OTHER SHEEP (John 10:16-21)

▶ Jesus alludes to the universal dimensions of His mission when He says, "I have other sheep that are not of this sheep pen" (v. 16). What "other sheep" is He speaking of?

▶ Here we see the missionary mandate of Jesus. His vision is to go to all the nations of the world, call out His sheep, and make them one flock. This is an enormous task because there are so many sheep pens. We are left with a puzzle. How will the Shepherd go to all the nations of the world if He has already given His life for the sheep of the first sheep pen? How do you solve the riddle?

5. I AND THE FATHER ARE ONE (John 10:22-42)

Here we have the figurative language of the Good Shepherd giving His life for the sheep made concrete. Those who do not believe in Him are the unwanted sheep.

The Jews demand that Jesus tell them plainly if He is the Christ. He does so in verse 30, and because of this they promptly attempt to kill Him. (I'm not sure I'd be willing to tell people who I was if every time I did so, they tried to kill me.) Jesus appeals to His miracles as a defense (v. 31), but the Jews reject this defense because they are not His sheep (v. 26).

▶ In verses 27 and 28, Jesus makes two promises to those who follow Him. What are they?

▶ Throughout John's Gospel, Jesus has emphasized His connection to the Father, but now He captures it succinctly with the phrase "I and the Father are one" (v. 30). Based upon your study of John up to this point, what does He mean by this?

▶ Jesus, in verses 34-38, presents several arguments to defend His claims. What are they?

Gods?

"'I have said you are gods'?" (v. 34).

Jesus cites Psalm 82:6 to defend His claim that He is God's Son. Jesus' argument runs, if God called them "gods" because they received the Word of God, shouldn't this apply even more to "the one whom the Father set apart as his very own and sent into the world" (v. 36)?

This is a tricky scripture to interpret. What did Jesus mean? Are all of us "gods"? The clue to the mystery is the role of the Word of God. To call those who obey the word "gods" is a merely a figure of speech. By receiving the Word of God, they became godlike. Simple enough.

So is Jesus saying He is just another obedient servant of the Word, but not really God? Yes and no. Yes, He is obedient. But no, He does not receive the Word—He is the Word. And that makes all the difference.

DISCOVERY GROUP

STUDY SCRIPTURE: John 10:1-42

KEY VERSE: John 10:11

Who Are You Going to Trust?

"Here come those nice Mormon missionaries," Stephanie's mother exclaimed. "They're so clean-cut and polite, and I just love their television commercials; they're so wholesome and family oriented."

That's how Stephanie started going to the local Church of Jesus Christ of Latter-day Saints with her mother. At first it seemed like a regular Christian church, but she noticed some differences. Initially, the differences seemed superficial. The church didn't have a pastor in the regular sense that her old church had a pastor. The services were run by different men in the church. She also noticed that they didn't seem to know the Bible very well. They used another book called the Book of Mormon, which they said was like the Bible—but "more accurate." They seemed to talk a lot about a man named Joseph Smith, whom they called a prophet.

But Stephanie really noticed a difference between her old church and her new one when she was being taken into membership. The ideas she heard sounded very strange, and she wasn't certain whether she believed them or not. They talked about how God was once like us and how someday we will all be like God. But they didn't mean it as Christians do. They meant that God wasn't always God, but that He got bigger and better until He is who He is now. And then when she was planning for her baptism, a woman asked her to make a list of all the people in her family who had died but were not Latter-day Saints so that they could be baptized too. Finally, Stephanie realized she was involved with a non-Christian religion. She decided to call her old pastor to ask him some questions.

The Good Shepherd

We live in a world where new religions seem to start every day. How do we know what is true? How do we know who to trust? Jesus called himself the "Good Shepherd" because He is trustworthy. Read His word picture of the Good Shepherd, and answer the following questions. By performing this exercise, you will learn the difference between who to trust and who not to trust.

Jesus speaks of three types of spiritual leaders. Read about them in the verses below, and write a brief character sketch describing them:

"Thieves and robbers" (vv. 8 and 10)

"The hired hand" (vv. 12-13)

"The Good Shepherd" (vv. 7-18)

Trusting Jesus

What does it mean to trust and follow Jesus, the Good Shepherd? Read Psalm 23. Now, in the space below, paraphrase this psalm into contemporary language. Think about your life and translate this psalm into your experience.

Interview a Modern Good Shepherd

We call pastors "pastor," which literally means "shepherd," because they fulfill the call of Jesus. They carry on the work of Jesus by gathering and leading the people of God. Because of this they have a unique perspective—they are called to see people as Jesus sees and loves them. Use the following questions to help you interview your pastor.

1. Pastor, in what way is your work like the work of a shepherd?

2. We call Jesus the "Good Shepherd"; what does that mean for your ministry?

3. What are the most difficult things you must do as a pastor?

4. What is the most rewarding part of being a shepherd?

5. If you could give advice to someone just starting in the pastorate, what would your advice be?

8 Life and Death

STUDY SCRIPTURE: John 11:1—12:50

KEY VERSE: "I am the resurrection and the life. He who believes in me will live, even though he dies; and whoever lives and believes in me will never die" (John 11:25-26).

PERSONAL DISCOVERY

1. OVERVIEW

From the beginning Jesus has promised eternal life to those who believe in Him. This is quite a promise. Death waits for us all, and He's not impatient, for He knows we will all pay Him a visit sooner or later. It wasn't always this way, though. The story of the Garden of Eden shows that death was not God's idea. It is the consequence of sin.

The raising of Lazarus is the pivotal point in the Gospel story. The tension between Jesus and the Jewish rulers has been building, and the stakes have been getting higher and higher. The whole Jewish nation seems to be on the edge of their seats, waiting for the next move. The raising of Lazarus forces the Jews to lay down their cards. Jesus proves He can deliver on His promise by raising a man from the dead. And the Jewish leaders? Well, let's just say they prove that they can kill.

▶ Death will come to us all; what are some ways people deal with death?

▶ Different religions have different ideas about death and its meaning; what do Christians believe concerning death?

▶ Because of the rise of teen suicide, it seems as though more and more teenagers view death as better than life. Why?

▶ Grieving for someone we have lost is human. Jesus wept for Lazarus just moments before He raised him from the dead. What does this teach us about helping people who have lost loved ones to death?

2. A BELOVED FRIEND (11:1-16)

The raising of Lazarus was the crowning sign of Jesus' ministry; it was proof positive that Jesus could deliver on His promises. It was not His greatest sign because it was more difficult than the others; all His signs were beyond human power to do. Signs are not judged upon their degree of difficulty as though Jesus were an Olympic high diver performing before a crowd. Signs are judged by how well they express the purpose and work of God. And none of Jesus' signs more plainly and forcefully express the mission of Jesus Christ than the raising of Lazarus. This is why it is the seventh sign, and why it has been saved for last.

▶ Verse 5 tells us that Jesus loved Lazarus, but verse 6 states that Jesus waited "two more days" before He went to him. Why?

▶ In verse 4 Jesus says, "This sickness will not end in death. No, it is for God's glory so that God's Son may be glorified through it." This should sound familiar to you. When did Jesus say something like this before?

▶ Verses 14 and 15 reveal Jesus' purposes. What were they?

3. KEEPING A PROMISE (11:17-44)

We all must trust somebody. We simply can't make it on our own. Trusting people means placing ourselves in their care. What makes a person trustworthy? Isn't it keeping promises? If someone makes a promise, only to break it, will we believe in them? Of course not. Throughout John's Gospel, Jesus has been asking people to believe in Him and His promise of eternal life. The time has come for Jesus to show He has the power to do what He has promised to do.

▶ Why does it make sense to trust your life to someone who has power over death?

▶ By reading the story, you can see that this sign has all the elements of a major spectacle. Why did this sign have potential to be heard throughout the whole region?

▶ In verse 26, Jesus asks Martha for a confession of faith before He raises Lazarus. Why do you think He did this?

▶ Verse 35, the shortest verse in the Bible, reads, "Jesus wept." Why did Jesus weep when He knew that in just moments He would raise Lazarus from the dead?

▶ Many people believe death is the end of the story of our lives. We see from this story that those who believe in Jesus look forward to eternal life. How should this reality influence us?

4. THE DEATH SENTENCE (11:45— 12:19)

Jesus, by raising Lazarus from the dead, has fully revealed His continuity with His Father. Now the Jewish leadership reveals what is within them. The evil has been there all along, but it took Jesus' steady persistence to flush it out. And because Jesus has been their primary irritant, He will feel the brunt of their wrath.

▶ In verse 48, the leaders reveal what is really bugging them. Why do they fear Jesus?

▶ Verses 49-52 record the prophecy of Caiaphas the high priest. Clearly Caiaphas did not know what he was really saying. The prophecy can be interpreted in two ways. What do you think Caiaphas meant and what do you think the prophecy really meant?

▶ What does Caiaphas' prophecy teach us about the sovereignty of God?

▶ Jesus waited for the Passover to allow the Jews to get at Him. (Remember the significance of the Passover from the feeding of the 5,000?) Mary anoints Jesus for burial in verse 3. How do we know this is what the anointing signified?

▶ Verse 8 is perhaps the most abused verse in the Bible. Often it is used by selfish Christians to weasel out of their responsibility to care for the poor. Why is this an abuse of this scripture?

5. JESUS CONCLUDES HIS PUBLIC MINISTRY (12:20-50)

Jesus' public ministry has come to an end. In verse 23 He sums it up: "The hour has come for the Son of Man to be glorified." He then tells His listeners that time is just about to run out—"You are going to have the light just a little while longer" (v. 35).

▶ This is Botany 101. In verse 24, Jesus says the death of one seed produces many seeds. When He says a seed "dies," He is speaking figuratively of planting a seed in the ground. When this happens, a plant emerges from the ground, and that plant produces even more seeds. How is Jesus' death for us like the death of a seed?

▶ Jesus indicates that His death will glorify God (vv. 27-28). Remember glorify means "shine" or "radiate." How will His death bring praise to God?

▶ Verses 47 and 48 explain Jesus' method of judgment. In your own words, explain what you think He means.

▶ Finally, Jesus explains one last time that His words are not His own. Whose are they and why should we believe them?

Glory!

"The hour has come for the Son of Man to be glorified" (12:23).

The closer Jesus comes to the end, the more He talks of glory and glorification. What is this glory business all about anyway?

Glory means to shine or be radiant. Remember, one of the metaphors for Jesus and His work is light. Glory and light are closely related notions. Somehow Jesus' death will be a radiant, light-giving event. It will shine and cause people to burst out in praise to God. Keep this idea of radiance in mind as you read John's Gospel.

DISCOVERY GROUP

STUDY SCRIPTURE: John 11:1—12:50

KEY VERSE: John 11:25-26

Death

Psychologists tell us that it is impossible to imagine our own death. This is because it lies outside the sphere of our experience. But before we have lived very long in this world, we will know someone who dies. That someone may be distant, like an aunt who lives in another part of the country; or that someone may be close, like a friend or a parent. So whether we can imagine our own death or not, before long we all know that death is real, and deep in the back of our own minds we know, sooner or later, we too shall die.

Remember a time when someone broke the news to you of a death. Use the space below to reflect upon it, to describe your feelings and how you coped with it.

Grief

Jesus took death seriously. The whole goal of His ministry was to defeat death. And He knew His Father would enable Him to do that. Yet, just before He raised Lazarus from the dead, the evangelist tells us, "Jesus wept" (11:35). It's a good thing that He wept. His weeping teaches us that it is OK to weep for those we lose to death.

● How does Jesus' grief help us understand our own grief?

● Jesus comforted Martha and Mary. In the light of this, what should Christians do for those who grieve?

Hope

The story of Jesus is a story of hope. Throughout his Gospel, John quotes Jesus again and again as He offers hope to those trapped in despair. Jesus does this by promising Eternal Life to all who believe in Him. When Jesus raised Lazarus from the dead, He proved He could deliver on His promise. With a Savior like this, we never have to despair because we know that no matter how bad it gets, hope will win! Let's do some hard thinking. How does the hope we have in Jesus help us when . . .

- we lose someone we love?

- our world seems like it is falling apart?

- all the news we hear is bad news?

- our friends, family, and even other Christians become cynical and negative about everything?

Joy

With our hope we have an irrepressible joy. It is a joy that, while respectful of death, knows death is not the end of the story. Our joy is found not in circumstances but in Jesus.

Here's a hymn written by Henry Van Dyke that expresses the joy we have in Jesus.

Joyful, Joyful, We Adore Thee

Joyful, joyful, we adore Thee, God of glory, Lord of love;
Hearts unfold like flow'rs before Thee, Opening to the sun above.
Melt the clouds of sin and sadness; Drive the dark of doubt away.
Giver of immortal gladness, Fill us with the light of day!

All Thy works with joy surround Thee; Earth and heav'n reflect Thy rays;
Stars and angels sing around Thee, Center of unbroken praise.
Field and forest, vale and mountain, Flowery meadow, flashing sea,
Chanting bird and flowing fountain Call us to rejoice in Thee!

Thou art giving and forgiving, Ever blessing, ever blest,
Wellspring of the joy of living, Ocean depth of happy rest!
Thou our Father, Christ our Brother—All who live in love are Thine.
Teach us how to love each other; Lift us to the joy divine!

Mortals join the mighty chorus Which the morning stars began.
Father-love is reigning o'er us; Brother-love binds man to man.
Ever singing, march we onward, Victors in the midst of strife.
Joyful music leads us sunward In the triumph song of life!

—Henry van Dyke

9 The Journey from Me to We

STUDY SCRIPTURE: John 13:1—14:31

KEY VERSE: "If you love me, you will obey what I command" (John 14:15).

PERSONAL DISCOVERY

1. OVERVIEW

Jesus has left the crowds behind and is now giving His last moments to His disciples. It's like being in the eye of a storm; conflict lies behind, and Jesus' final challenge lies ahead. Here the atmosphere, while intimate, is charged with energy. Every word is important, and every action is filled with meaning. The disciples, while uncertain how to interpret it all, are on the edge of their seats, waiting for the Lord to help them understand.

We are privileged eavesdroppers. What Jesus says to those who are with Him is intended for our ears too. What applies to them applies to us. Read the two chapters assigned with this session and answer the following questions:

▶ If you knew you were to die tomorrow, wouldn't you want to spend your last evening with your closest friends, discussing what is really important to you? This is what Jesus did. What are the things Jesus seemed to think important enough to discuss the last evening of His life?

▶ A leader's final commands are his most binding. List as many commands as you can find in this section.

▶ Jesus makes some promises to His disciples, which were doubly significant considering their timing. List as many promises as you can find.

2. FOOT WASHING (13:1-17)

The evening begins with an act that stunned the disciples. It certainly must
have turned everything upside down. Jesus washes feet. In that act, He placed
everything in perspective; every word He has spoken and every deed He has
done must now be understood as a service. And He places a burden upon His
followers, for as He says, "No servant is greater than his master." They must do
the same for each other because to refuse is to reject His teaching.

▶ Why did Jesus wash His disciples' feet? "Because they were dirty" is not
an acceptable answer. Why did He want them to serve one another?

▶ Some churches practice foot washing as a sacrament (like baptism and
Communion) to express a willingness to follow Jesus' example. Foot
washing was a common and necessary service in the ancient world.
What are ways Christians can serve today?

▶ At the very end of the lesson, in verse 17, Jesus tells His disciples, "Now
that you know these things, you will be blessed if you do them." What
could that mean? How can serving people be a blessing to the servant?

3. NIGHT (13:18-38)

Remember how Jesus kept telling His disciples that He had to work as long
as it was day? (5:17; 9:4-5; 11:9-10). Notice that as soon as Judas leaves, the
narrator says, "And it was night." It is night because, for a moment, evil is allowed to do its worst. During Jesus' public ministry it was day. Jesus, the Light
of the World, through His teaching and miraculous signs, spoke His Father's

words and did His Father's work. And with His light came life. Lame men walked, blind men saw, and dead men were raised. Now it is night, and the darkness will bring what it contains.

▶ Remember that throughout John's Gospel, bread symbolizes the body of Jesus. It is when Jesus gives Judas bread that Satan enters into him. For some reason Judas rejects Jesus and betrays Him. What are some reasons people reject the life of Jesus?

▶ Jesus almost seems relieved that Judas is gone. He says at this point, "Now is the Son of Man glorified and God is glorified in him." Remember that glory means to "shine" or "radiate." How has Jesus accomplished this?

▶ In verse 38 we see that, while Judas is the only disciple to betray Jesus, Peter will deny Him three times. Indeed all the disciples will desert Him; not one will speak up in His defense. Jesus stood completely alone; only His Father was with Him. His disciples are not the only ones to forsake Jesus, though. Throughout the long history of the Christian Church, denial has been the Church's greatest enemy. How do Christians still forsake the Lord today?

4. CONTINUITY (14:1-11)

From the beginning, Jesus emphasized His connectedness with His Father. The word He speaks is His Father's word (7:16), the works He does are His Father's works (5:19). All along He points to himself and declares that looking at Him is the same thing as looking at the Father. Apparently, Jesus did not screen the disciples at the door by their intelligence because they still seem to have a difficult time putting it all together. Here He drives the point home like a carpenter driving a nail.

▶ We have seen that the Jewish leaders had become corrupt and had blocked the channel of God's Word to the people. Rather than seeking to glorify God, they sought to glorify themselves (7:18); and rather than serve God, they served the devil (8:44). With this background, what is the significance of Jesus' words, "I am the way and the truth and the life" (14:6)?

▶ The word "way" would indicate that there is a "where." Jesus is the way to where? Jesus answers the question in verses 2 through 4. All along, each time Jesus has mentioned His destination He has added, "Where I am [going], you cannot come" (7:34). But that now changes. Where is Jesus going and why may the disciples come where others may not?

▶ When I was young, I was taught that in heaven we each would have a mansion if we were faithful to Jesus. In my mind's eyes I saw large, palatial estates for everyone. But the more I thought about it, the less attractive it all seemed. After all, it gets kind of lonely living in a big house all by yourself. But here Jesus speaks of "many rooms." Heaven is a single household with plenty of room in which we may live. Think about verses 2 through 4, and describe what you think life will be like in our Father's house.

5. JOIN THE CIRCLE (14:12-31)

While Jesus' connectedness with the Father has been the message of the first half of John's Gospel, the invitation to join in that continuity is the message of the second half. The fellowship Jesus enjoys with His Father is not something we are only to observe and envy for all eternity—no! We are invited to join the party! Jesus hinted at this in 13:20 and spoke more plainly in 14:2-4, but now He reaches out to the disciples and to us and says, "Join us!"

▶ In 14:2-4 we learn that we can anticipate participation in Christ's exaltation—we will be part of that wonderful heavenly household. But before we go up, we must go down. In 14:12 we see that we are to continue the work of Christ in the world after Jesus has gone. Based upon what you know of Jesus' relationship to His Father, what does "do what I have been doing" mean?

▶ In verses 15 through 31, Jesus says loving Him means obeying His commands. Carrying out His work is done by obedience, and love is our motivation. But is that all we are equipped with? Who else will join us and how will He help us continue the work of Jesus?

DISCOVERY GROUP

STUDY SCRIPTURE: John 13:1—14:31

KEY VERSE: John 14:15

How May I Serve You?

Not many of us will face the ordeal of dying for a friend, but we all must determine whether or not we will live for a friend. Living for others is called service. Jesus served His disciples by washing their feet, then He commanded them to do likewise. In this way they would follow the example of their Master.

Today foot washing might seem irrelevant, but service is always relevant. In the space below, brainstorm on all the possible ways you can think of serving others.

Who's on Top?

We live in a world where greatness is measured by how many people serve you. Those with the most money and power have the most servants, and because of this, we think they're great. But in the kingdom of God everything is upside down. Jesus says greatness is measured by how many you serve. In this section do an inventory of your relationships and ask the question, who's on top? In other words, am I being served or am I serving?

1. Family (list your family members here)

2. Friends (list your friends)

3. People from church

4. People from school

5. Your neighborhood

6. Your city

7. Your nation and world

Where's the Blessing?

In every church there is someone who is known as a great servant. Here's a chance to find out whether or not Jesus' promise that service will be blessed is true. Interview a servant. Ask them: how they started serving, why they serve, what lessons they've learned as a servant, what blessings they've received by serving, and whether or not they would recommend service for everybody.

I Want to Be like Jesus

Read and sing the words to the hymn printed below. Is this your desire? Is this song your testimony?

I have one deep, supreme desire—That I may be like Jesus.
To this I fervently aspire—That I may be like Jesus.
I want my heart His throne to be, So that a watching world may see
His likeness shining forth in me. I want to be like Jesus.

He spent His life in doing good; I want to be like Jesus.
In lowly paths of service trod; I want to be like Jesus.
He sympathized with hearts distressed; He spoke the words that cheered and blessed;
He welcomed sinners to His breast. I want to be like Jesus.

A holy, harmless life He led; I want to be like Jesus.
The Father's will—His drink and bread; I want to be like Jesus.
And when at last He comes to die, "Forgive them, Father," hear Him cry
For those who taunt and crucify. I want to be like Jesus.

Oh, perfect life of Christ my Lord! I want to be like Jesus.
My recompense and my reward—That I may be like Jesus.
His Spirit fill my hungering soul, His power all my life control.
My deepest prayer, my highest goal—That I may be like Jesus.

—Thomas O. Chisholm

10 No Greater Love

STUDY SCRIPTURE: John 15:1—16:33

KEY VERSE: "As the Father has loved me, so have I loved you. Now remain in my love" (John 15:9).

PERSONAL DISCOVERY

1. OVERVIEW

We are in the eye of a storm. Outside, the raging winds wait for Jesus to take His next step. But for now Jesus is engaged in the important work of transferring His ministry to His disciples.

"Unless a kernel of wheat falls to the ground and dies, it remains only a single seed. But if it dies, it produces many seeds" (12:24). Jesus is preparing His disciples to become the seeds of His ongoing ministry. It's all part of the divine plan. His death, rather than being an end, will be a new beginning, a birth of something new into the world. "A woman giving birth to a child has pain because her time has come; but when her baby is born she forgets the anguish because of her joy that a child is born into the world" (16:21).

We are allowed to eavesdrop on this intimate circle because as believers in Jesus we are part of the conspiracy. We, too, are seeds produced by the death of the one kernel of wheat. What does it mean to continue the ministry of Jesus in the world?

▶ Briefly summarize what you learned from the last session.

▶ By reading this session's assigned scripture, do you see any themes that carry over from the previous session?

▶ Are any new themes introduced?

2. LOVE (15:1-17)

In chapter 14, Jesus invited His disciples to join the circle of His fellowship with the Father by means of the Holy Spirit. He tells them that when they receive the Spirit, "You will realize that I am in my Father, and you are in me, and I am in you" (14:20). The intimacy and closeness of it all seems very attractive. But warm fuzzies are not the purpose. In chapter 15, Jesus uses a powerful figure of speech to help His followers understand the meaning of it all. This portion sums up the purpose of our "remaining in the vine."

▶ What happens to those branches that do not bear fruit?

▶ Jesus speaks of the Father pruning branches that do bear fruit (v. 2*b*). What do you think this means?

▶ What is fruit? What acts or words result in glory for the Father? (Hint: Look at verses 9-14 for Jesus' own explanation.)

▶ In verse 15, Jesus elevates the status of the disciples from "servants" to "friends." What is the difference between a servant and a friend according to Jesus?

3. HATE (15:18—16:4)

The connectedness of the disciples with Jesus and His work is complete. It will include both the unpleasant as well as the pleasant parts. In verse 20, Jesus says, "Remember the words I spoke to you: 'No servant is greater than his master.'" He warns His disciples that if they are faithful, the world will hate them for the same reason it hated Him.

▶ Those whom the world hates do not stand alone. If the world hates the disciples—who else does it hate in the process?

▶ Because evil is a big zero, it needs truth and life to sustain it. It is a parasite. It must lie to prop itself up, and every lie needs a bit of truth to make it believable. Jesus tells His disciples, "A time is coming when anyone who kills you will think he is offering a service to God" (16:2). How did the Jewish leaders believe they were offering a service to God by killing Jesus?

▶ Can you think of other times and places that great evil was done in the name of God?

4. THE HOLY SPIRIT (16:5-16)

The One who binds us to Jesus and makes us part of His work is the Holy Spirit. In 14:26, Jesus tells us that the Spirit will testify to us so that we may testify to the world. Now Jesus helps us understand the ministry of the Spirit in greater depth.

▶ Jesus tells us He will send the Spirit to the disciples (v. 7) so that what may happen?

▶ Verses 13-15 speak of what the Spirit will do among the disciples. What will He do and how will His work help the disciples continue Jesus' work?

5. JOY (16:17-33)

Jesus begins to prepare the disciples for the trial they will soon be facing. Read the following verses and paraphrase (put in your own words) Jesus' words of comfort.

▶ vv. 20-22

▶ vv. 23-27

▶ v. 28

▶ v. 33

While what the disciples (not to mention Jesus) are about to experience is painful, the pain will be short-lived, and the end result will bring them joy. Using what you have read and written, explain why the sacrifice of Jesus on our behalf should bring us joy.

DISCOVERY GROUP

STUDY SCRIPTURE: John 15:1—16:33

KEY VERSE: John 15:9

Just Imagine

Imagine, just for a moment, that you are someone famous. It could be anybody—someone in the entertainment industry or in sports or perhaps even politics, like the president of the United States. Now imagine that you, in your new identity, live in your house and go to your school and attend church at your church. Now here's the big question. How do you act around your friends and family and how do these people respond to you?

Who are you? _____

How does your best friend treat you and how do you treat your best friend?

How about your mother?

How about your pastor?

Your English teacher?

● Now apply this activity to living the Christian life. How would truly having Jesus' identity inside of you change the way you look at yourself and relate to others?

In Jesus' Name

Jesus tells His disciples that they are an extension of His life in the world. That's what the vine and the branches imagery is all about. Jesus' disciples live in the name of Jesus, doing His work and speaking His words to the glory of His Father. Based on the scripture we're studying in this session, what are our rights and responsibilities as Christians?

When you live in Jesus' name, what are your rights?

When you live in Jesus' name, what are your responsibilities?

No Greater Love

The little missionary orphanage hadn't hurt anybody, but in war that doesn't matter. If a bomb falls on you by mistake, tough luck. The missionaries and a few of the children were killed instantly, but many others lay wounded and dying.

People from the Vietnamese village radioed for help and reached American military forces. An American navy doctor and a nurse were sent in a jeep to help. When they arrived, they surveyed the scene and determined that a little eight-year-old girl would die without an immediate blood transfusion. The doctor and nurse checked their own blood, but neither had the right type. Several of the orphan children did, however.

The doctor spoke a little Vietnamese and the nurse a little French. Using both languages plus some impromptu sign language, they tried to explain to the children that unless they could replace some of the girl's lost blood, she would die. They asked the children if anyone would be willing to give blood to help.

The children sat in wide-eyed silence. After several moments, a small hand slowly and waveringly went up, dropped back down, and then went up again.

"Oh, thank you," the nurse said in French. "What's your name?"

"Heng," the little boy replied.

She quickly placed Heng on a pallet and swabbed his arm with alcohol and inserted a needle in his vein. Through this ordeal Heng lay still and silent.

After a minute, he let out a shuddering sob, quickly covering his face with his free hand. "Is it hurting, Heng?" the doctor asked. Heng shook his head, but after a few moments another sob escaped. The doctor asked him again if the needle hurt, but Heng shook his head. But his sobs gave way to steady, silent crying, his eyes screwed tight and his fist in his mouth to stifle his sobs. The doctor and nurse were concerned. Something was very wrong. At this point a Vietnamese nurse arrived and seeing Heng's distress, quickly spoke to him in Vietnamese. Listening to his answer, she calmed him with a soothing voice. After a moment Heng stopped crying and looked at the Vietnamese nurse. When she nodded, a look of great relief spread over his face.

Turning to the Americans, the nurse said, "He thought he was dying. He misunderstood what you wanted. He thought you wanted all of his blood so that the little girl could live."

"But why would he be willing to do that?" asked the American nurse.

The Vietnamese nurse repeated the question to the little boy, who answered simply, "She's my friend."*

Motto

"I have been crucified with Christ and I no longer live, but Christ lives in me. The life I live in the body, I live by faith in the Son of God, who loved me and gave himself for me" (Galatians 2:20).

---

*From, "No Greater Love," *Missileer,* newspaper for Patrick Air Force Base, Fla., February 13, 1987.

11. Who Needs Church?

STUDY SCRIPTURE: John 17:1-26

KEY VERSE: "I have given them the glory that you gave me, that they may be one as we are one: I in them and you in me. May they be brought to complete unity to let the world know that you sent me and have loved them even as you have loved me" (John 17:22-23).

PERSONAL DISCOVERY

1. OVERVIEW

This is a critical point in the story of Jesus. For three years He has given himself to His disciples. He has revealed the Father to them in a way never seen before, and now He is about to leave them. Unless the disciples remember what they have witnessed, and unless they in turn witness to others, the light of Jesus will fade and be lost from the world.

Jesus wants His work to continue. Remember, He has sheep in other pens to call out. (See chapter 10.) Without His disciples to continue His work, how will they be gathered into one fold?

In a relay race, the passing of the baton is the most critical moment. If the baton is dropped, the race is lost. Jesus is entrusting His work to this ragtag bunch. You can almost sense His concern. But He is not trusting them alone, for He knows what is in the hearts of men. He is entrusting both His work and His disciples to the Father. Chapter 17 is His prayer for them and for us.

▶ If you knew you were soon to die, like within the next 24 hours, you'd probably spend a lot of time in prayer. What would you pray for?

▶ Contrast what you would pray for with what Jesus prayed for. In what ways are your prayers the same and in what ways do they differ?

▶ What does His prayer tell you about Jesus' priorities?

2. GLORIFY ME (17:1-5)

Notice, Jesus is praying in the presence of His disciples. He wants them, and us, to hear His prayer. He begins the prayer with a sort of review, a kind of mission statement that reads, "You granted [me] authority over all people that [I] might give eternal life to all those you have given [me]." Jesus then goes on to define what eternal life is in verse 3. Summarize it in your own words.

▶ Eternal life is impossible without knowing God, and knowing God is impossible without knowing Jesus Christ. This is why Jesus said, "I am the way and the truth and the life. No one comes to the Father except through me" (14:6). How has Jesus given us the knowledge of God?

▶ Glorify means to "shine" or "radiate." Jesus reminds the Father that He has brought Him glory. How has the work of Jesus brought glory to the Father?

▶ Now Jesus asks His Father to lift Him up. How do you think the Father will accomplish this?

3. I HAVE REVEALED YOU (17:6-10)

Here we see just what Jesus has entrusted to His disciples. Remember the Good Shepherd metaphor in chapter 10? Here we see it again. He has called out those who have chosen to do God's will (7:17) and has revealed the Father to them (v. 6). It is this revelation that must be preserved in the world.

▶ Jesus reminds the Father that the disciples, although they have been entrusted to Jesus, belong to the Father. Which verses communicate this thought?

▶ Earlier you imagined the Father glorifying the Son. Now notice in verse 10 that Jesus has received glory through His disciples. How do the followers of Jesus glorify the Son?

4. PROTECT THEM (17:11-19)

Now Jesus entrusts the disciples to the Father's care. He received them from the Father (v. 6), as a Good Shepherd He protected them while He was in the world (v. 10), and now He is returning them to the Father's care (v. 11). Why is Jesus so concerned for the welfare of His followers?

▶ Jesus asks the Father to protect them in two ways. What are they? (Hint: see verses 11 and 17.)

▶ Jesus asks the Father to sanctify His disciples. "Sanctify" means "to separate" or "set apart." It's easy to see how separation from the world can protect you from the world. But Jesus says, "My prayer is not that you take them out of the world" (v. 15). He then goes on to say, "I have sent them into the world" (v. 18). The separation from the world is not a physical separation, but a spiritual one. How is this spiritual separation accomplished? (Hint: see verse 17.)

▶ Why is our protection in the world spiritual and not physical?

5. THAT THE WORLD MAY BELIEVE (17:20-26)

Jesus prays for people like you and me. Jesus' concern is that something happens among us so that the world may believe His Father sent Him. What is that something? (See verse 23.)

▶ In chapter 10 Jesus says that the unity of His flock is a big concern of His, and again in chapter 13 He says, "By this all men will know that you are my disciples, if you love one another" (v. 35). The message here seems to be that the unity of Jesus' followers is the key to revealing the glory of God to the world. How does the Church seem to be doing in this area?

▶ When you think of your own local church, does it seem to be a place of love and unity?

▶ What are some of the things that keep the church from being the kind of place Jesus wants it to be?

In the Name of Jesus

In the preceding chapters Jesus tells His disciples to "ask in my name" (14:13; 15:16; and 16:23-24). Now He asks the Father to protect them by the power of the same name (v. 11). It's difficult for us to understand what this means because we live in such a self-centered and individualistic culture. In ancient times it was common for people to ask in the name of others. If someone of power and prominence entrusted their name to you, by the power of their name you had the authority to act on their behalf and enjoy the privileges they enjoyed. Jesus entrusted His name to His disciples. By His name they may come to the Father, and by that same name they enjoy the Father's protection.

DISCOVERY GROUP

STUDY SCRIPTURE: John 17:1-26

KEY VERSE: John 17:22-23

No Salvation Outside the Church

The Church is the most important institution in the world because she has been entrusted with the message of Jesus Christ. It is the mission of the Church to remember and experience God's glory and let it shine in the world. Without the Church, no one would know about Jesus because people don't learn about Jesus by looking inside themselves. They learn about Jesus by looking inside the Church.

Jesus told His disciples that His glory will shine in the world as they do certain things. Look up the following verses and describe what these things are.

13:34-35

16:5-15

17:20-26

Doing Church

At your church, the people of God are to work to make Jesus' vision a reality. The different things that happen on a Sunday and throughout the week are designed to make it happen. Below are listed certain practices most churches have in common. Give the pastor or the assistant pastor of your church a call and interview him or her over the phone. With what you've learned about Jesus' vision for the church in mind, ask your pastor to describe how these various ministries of the church are designed to make Jesus' vision a reality.

Worship

1. "What is the purpose of the worship service?"

2. "How does worship promote love for God and love for people?"

3. "What advice would you give for experiencing worship most fully?"

Sunday School

1. "What is the purpose of Sunday School?"

2. "What is the role of the Holy Spirit in our Sunday School?"

3. "What is your vision for the Sunday School of our church?"

Fellowship

1. "What is the purpose of the fellowship of our church?"

2. "How can the teens make our fellowship more effective?"

3. "What are we doing through our fellowship to help the hurting and lonely of our community?"

Final Question

"What can I do as a teen to contribute to the life and witness of our church?"

Knocking Down the Walls

Because unity is so important to the witness of the Church, our enemies work overtime to divide us. Below are a list of personal and social barriers that keep the Church from bearing a unified witness for Jesus in our world. Prayerfully think of ways we as Christians can overcome these barriers.

Personal Walls

1. Unforgiving spirit

2. Gossip

3. Selfishness

4. Egotism

5. Others?

Social Barriers

1. Racism

2. Denominationalism

3. Economics

4. Others?

Praying with Jesus

Read Jesus' prayer again, particularly the last portion (vv. 20-26). Now, with Jesus' thoughts in your heart, write a prayer to the Father that reflects the prayer of Jesus.

12 Lift High the King

STUDY SCRIPTURE: John 18:1—19:42

KEY VERSE: "'You are a king, then!' said Pilate. Jesus answered, 'You are right in saying I am a king. In fact, for this reason I was born, and for this I came into the world, to testify to the truth. Everyone on the side of truth listens to me'" (John 18:37).

PERSONAL DISCOVERY

1. OVERVIEW

Everything in the Gospel of John has been building to this moment. How ironic—Jesus, a man who deserved life and praise, was given death and shame by the very people He came to save. Viewed from one side, it seems like the ultimate disappointment—a tragedy in a tragic world, an ending where the bad guys live happily ever after. But viewed from the other side, the heavenly side, it is hope and victory. Jesus submits to the whole process without resistance because it has been His end to die from the beginning. He does not seek justice; justice would ruin everything. He desires to die a just man in an unjust way. This is the only way the plan will work. For the salvation He brings is a salvation by grace. By dying justly, He makes a way for all who know they are unjust to live.

▶ As you read the events surrounding our Lord's death, record the manner of His unjust treatment.

▶ Notice that He was despised and rejected. Record examples of how He was rejected by those who had the power to save His life.

▶ No doubt you've heard the story of Jesus' crucifixion many times before. Have you internalized its meaning? He died for us all. How has His death made a difference in your life?

2. WHO WILL BE A WITNESS FOR MY LORD? (18:1-27)

It is night, and they are coming for Jesus. He has been evading capture for three years, but the time has come to die, and He is going to make it easy for His persecutors to do Him in. In verse 2 we see that Jesus went where He knew Judas could find Him. When the mob approaches, He steps out and surrenders himself to them.

▶ His treatment by the Jews is worth some attention. When the mob called for Him in verse 5, Jesus answered, "I am." If you have the NIV, it reads "I am he." But you need to know that the original Greek did not use the pronoun "he." It simply reads "I am." Why is this important? (Look up these passages and try and figure it out for yourself: Exodus 3:13-14 and John 8:58-59.)

▶ By identifying himself with God, Jesus lets the Jews know they are not simply condemning a man named Jesus. Who are they ultimately condemning?

▶ According to Jewish law, a man could not be condemned without two incriminating witnesses. Jesus asks the high priest to produce His witnesses in verse 21. The high priest produces none. But there were two witnesses near who could have vindicated Jesus. Who were they?

▶ Why did Peter and the beloved disciple remain silent when they could have spoken up?

▶ The trial of Jesus continues today. Jesus presents himself to the world for judgment as long as this world shall last. The world condemns Him without proof, but Jesus has many witnesses who could vindicate Him. Have you been a witness for the Lord this week?

3. THE KING OF TRUTH (18:28—19:16)

Because dealing with Jesus was a hot potato, the Jews didn't want to do Him in themselves. So they went to Pilate for a favor. When Pilate asks them for a charge, the Jews respond, "Trust us, the guy's a criminal" (v. 30). Pilate, being an astute politician, smells something fishy and tells the Jews to judge Jesus for themselves. Since the Jews want to keep their hands clean, they give Pilate a strong nudge, "We want you to kill Him for us" (v. 31). So Pilate is stuck with the problem of finding a way to kill an innocent man. He begins with a hunch. Political revolutionaries were common in Palestine; he had one in jail that very moment (v. 40). If he could charge Jesus with political subversion, he could have Him killed.

▶ Pilate asks Jesus, "Are you the king of the Jews?" (v. 33). Jesus' answer must have surprised and, in a way, disappointed Pilate. Why?

▶ According to verse 37, Jesus is a king, but a different kind of King. What is Jesus the King of?

▶ What does Pilate's response in verse 38 tells us about him?

- ▶ Apparently Pilate saw the "King of the Jews" ploy as the best way to dispose of Jesus. By tagging Jesus as a revolutionary, he had the ability to vindicate himself and trick the Jews into renouncing their own nationalistic aspirations. Pilate was a subtle character and a cunning politician. How did he use the title "King of the Jews" to railroad Jesus to the Cross?

- ▶ What does the Sanhedrin's treatment of Jesus tell us about their attitude toward truth?

- ▶ Pilate's final moments with Jesus must have been an eye-opener for him. Jesus places everything in perspective when He says, "You would have no power over me if it were not given to you from above" (19:11). How does this help us understand the Crucifixion?

4. THE CRUCIFIXION (19:17-27)

Considering that the whole Gospel story is intended to bring us to this point, the account of the Crucifixion itself is surprisingly short. It is enough for us to know that Jesus died on a cross in fulfillment of prophecy. But there's irony—two opposite ways of looking at the same thing. From early in His ministry Jesus has spoken of being "lifted up." And at last He is on a cross.

- ▶ How can the Cross at one moment be understood in two ways?

- ▶ Another element of irony in this passage is the sign nailed to the Cross by Pilate. It read, "JESUS OF NAZARETH, THE KING OF THE JEWS" (v. 19). What do you think this sign meant for Pilate? And finally for Jesus' disciples?

5. DEATH AND BURIAL (19:28-42)

At this point in the narrative the author wants us to know two things. First, Jesus died according to prophecy, and second, Jesus did in fact die. It was difficult for Jews to open their minds to a crucified Messiah. It seemed to contradict everything they had longed and hoped for. So, showing Jews that the very scriptures they believed in told of a suffering Messiah was very important.

▶ What are the particular elements of the story that are noted as fulfillment of prophecy?

▶ After the Christian movement gained momentum and had produced many followers of Jesus among the Jews, detractors of the Church began to claim that Jesus had never really died at all; the whole thing was an enormous hoax. How did the author prove that Jesus did in fact die?

▶ Even though 2,000 years have passed, and Christians have taken the time and effort to document these facts, many people still reject that Jesus died in fulfillment of prophecy. Why is this so?

DISCOVERY GROUP

STUDY SCRIPTURE: John 18:1—19:42

KEY VERSE: John 18:37

The Blood of Jesus

In the 16th century, King Philip II of Spain, a Roman Catholic, ruled over Holland. He hated the Dutch Protestants and had thousands of them tortured, maimed, imprisoned, and exiled for the slightest crimes. When they finally rose up in defiance, he decided to get tough and sent a Spanish army to crush the insurrection.

The city of Rotterdam fought valiantly for a while but was finally swept over by a victorious Spanish army. The conquerors went from house to house, ferreting out the citizens and slaughtering them wholesale in the streets. Men, women, children, the aged, it didn't matter. King Philip wanted the Dutch punished for their insolence. In one house, though, a group of families huddled together, fear gripping their hearts as the Spanish approached.

Suddenly a young man had an idea. He took a young goat belonging to the household, killed it, then with a broom swept its blood beneath the door of the house. Waiting breathlessly, they heard the booted feet of the Spanish soldiers stop at the door. Soon the Spaniards were battering the door. Then they heard one of them say, "Look at the blood! Well, men, looks like our work has already been done. Come away!" Their footsteps faded as they went to do their killing elsewhere. The household had been saved by the blood of a goat.

How is the story of Jesus, "the Lamb of God," similar to this one?

Learning How to Die

Jesus was ready to die because He had had plenty of practice. Every time He said yes to His Father and no to himself, He died a death that prepared Him for His final death. Jesus' death atones for our sins, but it also sets an example for us. Are you struggling to obey God? Use this space to write about some of your struggles to obey, and think of ways Jesus' example can give you the strength you need to follow Him.

Martyrdom

Martyr comes from the Greek word *martus*, which means "to witness." It's interesting to note that witnessing came to be understood as synonymous with dying for what you believe. The reason neither Peter nor the "beloved disciple" witnessed for Jesus on the night of His trial is because they were afraid to die. Being afraid to witness is still a matter of being afraid to die.

Being afraid to die is normal, and so is being afraid to witness. Listed below are some of the more common reasons people fear witnessing. Go through the list and write out different ways people can overcome these fears.

1. Inadequate knowledge of the Bible

2. Bad experiences witnessing in the past

3. Possibility of rejection

4. Social disapproval

5. Lack of an up-to-date experience with God

Gratitude

For those who believe in Jesus, the whole Christian life is a life of gratitude. We give our lives to God because Jesus gave His life for us. Use this space to write a prayer of thankfulness for the sacrifice of Jesus.

13 The Future

STUDY SCRIPTURE: John 20:1—21:25

KEY VERSE: "Again Jesus said, 'Peace be with you! As the Father has sent me, I am sending you.' And with that he breathed on them and said, 'Receive the Holy Spirit. If you forgive anyone his sins, they are forgiven; if you do not forgive them, they are not forgiven'" (John 20:21-23).

PERSONAL DISCOVERY

1. OVERVIEW

The night has passed and the dawn has come! There has been no light since Judas left Jesus and the disciples in chapter 13. From then until Resurrection morning, darkness reigned and evil did its worst. But night is past, and the pain and grief of Jesus' trial and crucifixion are over. From now on light will increase and grow.

This means the future belongs to the one true God and His Christ. A new world is coming, and heaven itself will be made new; and the kingdoms of this world shall become the kingdom of God, and this Kingdom shall never end (Revelation 11:15). How can we know for certain? Why, the Resurrection, of course! It is the firstfruits of the renewal of all things. As Jesus died for all, He was raised for all, and the power of that event will fill the universe.

▶ How does reading chapters 20 and 21 make you feel?

▶ Our world seems obsessed with gloom and doom predictions or with giddy and naive visions of a technological wonderland in the future. But we are Christians. When we look ahead, we don't predict tomorrow by the headlines of the newspaper or by whether or not our candidate is elected president. We view it through the window of Scripture. What kind of tomorrow does the Resurrection promise us?

2. THE EARLY APPEARANCES (John 20:1-29)

John records four appearances of Jesus for us after the Resurrection. By reading other portions of the New Testament, we know this is not all. But these episodes are recorded because each one bears its own message.

▶ Jesus appeared first to Mary Magdalene (vv. 10-18). The fact that He appeared first to a woman is highly significant. In the ancient world the testimony of a woman was not valid. But since this event, the fortunes of women have changed, and credit should go to Jesus for that. But another feature of this appearance is worthy of thought. Mary did not recognize Jesus until He spoke her name. If you have recognized Jesus as the resurrected Lord, you know it is not because you are so smart and perceptive; it is because Jesus has called you by name. How has this encounter changed your life?

▶ Jesus' second appearance was to His disciples (vv. 19-23). At this appearance He picks up where He left off before His trial and crucifixion. What does Jesus command His disciples to do? And what does He give to them?

▶ The third appearance is made especially for a doubting disciple (vv. 24-31). Doubting Thomas, poor guy, he'll never live this incident down. Sometimes people have doubts. If they are honest doubts, Jesus will address them. If you have doubts regarding Jesus' message, record them here and offer them to God. If they are genuine, let the story of Thomas comfort you.

▶ The message of Thomas' encounter with the Lord is that it is more blessed to not see and yet believe than to see and believe. Why does this manner of faith honor God?

3. THE MIRACULOUS CATCH OF FISH (John 21:1-14)

Each sign prior to the Crucifixion pointed toward Jesus' impending death, but since this one comes after, it illustrates what is to come after the Resurrection. As you read the story, remember every detail has meaning in the larger picture. Note some of the more important features. First, they are fishing at night and they catch nothing. Then in the morning they see Jesus. He tells them to cast their net on the right side of the boat—and presto! They catch more than a boatload of fish!

▶ What do you suppose the meaning of this sign is? Here are some clues regarding the main elements: (1) fishing = evangelism; (2) night = before the Resurrection; (3) morning = after the Resurrection; and (4) the right side of the boat = those whom God has called. Now let's see what you can make of this; and remember the sign is intended to look forward.

4. GRACE (John 21:15-19)

This is a wonderful story with which to conclude the Gospel because it so aptly illustrates the power of grace. It is the restoration and commission of Peter. Here we see some interesting parallels to the scene where Peter betrayed the Lord in chapter 18.

▶ How many things can you find that are the same?

▶ There are also some interesting differences. In fact, some things are precisely the opposite of what they were during Peter's betrayal. What features might be called mirror images?

▶ Here is a summary of the two previous questions: The fire is the same, and so is the presence of Peter, the beloved disciple, and Jesus. Three features mirror those of the denial: then it was night, now it is day; then Peter denied Jesus three times, now he affirms Him three times; then Jesus died for Peter, but now Jesus tells Peter he will die for Him. How does this story provide us with hope for our own new beginnings?

5. CONCLUSION (John 20:30-31 and 21:22-25)

Now the writer brings his narrative to its conclusion. He does so by noting the inadequacy of his work (21:25) and by giving the reason for his writing (20:30-31). And he gives us his testimony that what he has written is true (21:24).

▶ How has reading this story of Jesus helped you believe?

▶ By reading this Gospel, how have you changed?

▶ Having believed and been changed, how can you testify to what you have seen and heard?

DISCOVERY GROUP

STUDY SCRIPTURE: John 20:1—21:25

KEY VERSE: John 20:21-23

It's a Whole New World

Because Jesus rose from the dead, life wins! This means that the world has a happy ending. Ever since Adam, death has had its way, but now its days are numbered. Some day death will die, and all creation will be released from decay. This means Christians are people of hope. We are fundamentally optimistic about the future.

- What do you believe the future holds?

- How much are your views shaped by God's Word?

The Future Isn't Science Fiction

Everybody needs hope, even people who don't believe in God. But when you don't have God to trust for the future, you look to something else. These days, people look to science fiction. And the most popular science fiction show of all time is "Star Trek."

Probably the most appealing thing about the show is the hope it offers. But we're Christians, and Christians don't watch television to find hope. Christians look to God—and God has given us His vision of the future in the Bible. Turn to Revelation, chapters 21 and 22. Read about the end of the world and in the space below, in your own words, describe what you see.

A New Life

In Revelation 21 and 22 you read about the renewal of all things and about a new heaven and a new earth. But what about you? What's your future? As a Christian, where do you fit in? Since you are a believer in Jesus, you will also participate in His new creation. Turn to 1 Corinthians 15 for a description of what you can anticipate.

Read 1 Corinthians 15:35-58 and answer the following questions:

- vv. 36-38: Paul says that our body is like a seed. Who does this remind you of?

- vv. 39-44: Here Paul describes a spiritual body. What is a spiritual body like?

- v. 58: Because we have this hope, what should we do?

The Great Commission

In John 20:21-23, Jesus commissions His disciples to continue His work in the field. We are also included in this Great Commission. We have been sent; we have the Holy Spirit; we have been given the authority to forgive sins. Let's do it. In the space below write a prayer of commitment and give yourself to Jesus and His Great Commission!